Run mee

CW00400609

Learn how to run meetings efficiently and effectively

Kate Keenan

Pocket Manager Books

Published by Pocket Manager
Regency House
2 Wood Street
Bath BA1 2JQ

www.kate-keenan.com

ISBN 978-1-909179-48-6

Previously published as The Management Guide to Running
Meetings by Oval Books.

Images are reproduced by kind permission of Oval Projects Ltd.

Original series editor – Anne Tauté, Oval Books
Editor – Catriona Tulloch Scott
Project manager – Clare Christian, The Book Guru
Book and cover re-design – Philip Jansseune, Walker Jansseune
Image enhancement – Matt Holland, MiH Design
Author photograph – Marko Dutka, Studio Marko

Cover: A sure sign of an effective meeting is when the coffee goes
cold in the cups.

Contents

This book is dedicated to
those who would like to manage better
but are too busy to begin.

Run meetings

Everyone agrees that positive and productive outcomes are the key objectives of any meeting. Unfortunately, many people say that a large proportion of the meetings they attend are futile and achieve little if anything at all.

Yet running meetings productively and efficiently is a relatively straightforward process. Even if you have never run one before, doing a little preparation in advance and being prepared to take control of the proceedings will go a long way to ensuring that the meeting achieves its overall purpose.

Whether you chair a local committee, run regular business meetings or find yourself having to referee family gatherings, knowing what you are doing will greatly enhance your confidence and improve the outcomes.

This book shows you how to run meetings well and helps you to make sure you get the best out of them. It offers simple, effective ways of making certain that any meetings you run will be considered worthwhile by those who attend them.

1 Why meetings do not work

Achieving anything often means that a meeting may be required to set the direction and make decisions. Yet the general opinion of meetings is often, *'That was a complete waste of time.'* This is a sentiment frequently voiced by those who have participated in meetings which were badly organised and lacked control.

Here are some the things you may have heard people say after a meeting , or maybe even said yourself:

- *'I might just as well not have been there.'* This suggests that there was little chance to contribute.
- *'It had nothing to do with me.'* This indicates that people felt excluded from the decisions that were made.
- *'All my points were criticised.'* This implies that the speaker did not get a fair hearing.
- *'I didn't see much point in meeting in the first place.'* This denotes that the purpose of the meeting was not clear.
- *'I was only there to make up the numbers.'* This hints that the outcome was considered to be a foregone conclusion.

All too often meetings get a bad press, resulting in discontent. This may be because the meeting was run in a way that the people attending never had a chance to contribute to the debate or participate in decisions.

Poor management

For meetings to be effective, they require direction. If there is no nominated individual to manage the proceedings in an orderly way, meetings can either wander aimlessly or become unruly, with no appreciable result. If it is not recognise that a level of firm control is required, behaviour may rapidly deteriorate.

On the other hand, if the individuals running the meeting are not experienced or do not understand what is expected of them, they may not be capable of exerting their influence so as to keep the meeting on track. It is essential that people know they need to:

- **Keep to an agenda** This guides the proceedings to a conclusion, so that people do not become irritated or consider the meeting unproductive.
- **Encourage all points of view** Each person attending needs to have an opportunity to express an opinion and does not end up feeling excluded and resentful.
- **Control the discussion** There needs to be time allowed for views to be considered and talk does not linger too long on one point.
- **Wind up the meeting with a proper summary** There needs to be a clear statement of what was achieved and what tasks people have to do as a result.
- **Record what was decided** This ensures there can be no misunderstandings or excuses at the next meeting.

It is often the lack of direction in a meeting and the lack of opportunity to have a 'say' which causes people to conclude that many meetings are a waste of time and effort.

Lack of structure

Meetings are often in trouble even before they begin because no-one has prepared an agenda listing the items to be discussed.

A meeting which takes place without a clearly defined structure is likely to create more problems than it solves. For instance:

- Those who attend will not be able to prepare, so will not have the required information to hand.
- With no time constraints the meeting will conclude when people run out of steam, get bored or have to leave.
- The same topic will be gone over several times while other items, often more important, will not brought up at all.
- There will be uncertainty about why the meeting was called or what purpose it has.

If people do not know exactly what needs to be deliberated at the meeting, they will not be able to participate positively. They will also not have had the opportunity to prepare what they want to say beforehand. This means discussion will almost certainly veer off at various tangents, so the meeting will almost certainly not achieve its objective.

Not valuing the meeting

The attitude people have to a meeting plays a large part in determining whether or not it will be worthwhile. Some of the signs that the meeting is not valued can include:

- Sending an uninformed substitute because the meeting is not thought to be important enough.
- Not having done what should have been done before the meeting.
- Accepting messages or receiving phone calls during the meeting.
- Not bringing the necessary information or notes needed for the meeting.

Sometimes the wrong people are at the meeting, and at other times, the right people fail to attend. People have even been known to turn up for the wrong meeting. How long it takes them to realise it is the wrong meeting, if at all, will depend on how well the meeting is being run and controlled.

To achieve productive results, it is essential to ensure that the right people attend the right meeting, that they have properly prepared for it and turn up in the right frame of mind.

Uncomfortable conditions

People find it difficult to make an intelligent contribution at any meeting if the venue for the meeting is not comfortable. Poor conditions can end up being the focus of attention, rather than the matter in hand.

It is as difficult to concentrate fully when the discussion continues for too long without a break as it is when there are constant interruptions or when people talk amongst themselves.

All these things mean the issues will not be given people's undivided attention, and the net result is that the meeting usually ends up being far less productive than it should be.

No need for the meeting

A meeting takes time and effort, yet people often call one simply because they have not considered any suitable alternatives which could provide the same results.

Gathering people together can provide a certain 'comfort' factor, a familiar way of doing things, so it goes on happening even when it may be unnecessary.

Meetings can also be used as a way of delaying making decisions or possibly avoiding taking personal responsibility.

It is always useful to take a step back and question what exactly the meeting is for, or even whether there is any need for it at all.

Usefulness of meetings

Meetings are always a means to an end; they are never an end in themselves. The conclusion of a meeting is usually just the beginning for other activities, even if it is simply the setting up of another meeting.

By regarding meetings as a constructive way of making decisions and the start of getting things done, you will find it much easier to direct your efforts. This means that the purpose for which the meeting was called is more likely to be achieved.

Questions to ask yourself

Think about your attitude to meetings and answer the following questions:

- Have I ever thought, *'That meeting was a waste of time?'*

- Have I ever felt despondent at the prospect of attending a meeting?

- Have I attended chaotic meetings?

- Have I been at a meeting where I was not quite clear about my reason for being there?

- Have I gone to a meeting and not given it my full attention?

- Have I sometimes felt that a meeting could be better organised?

- Have I ever wondered why a meeting was called in the first place?

If you have answered 'Yes' to several or most of these questions, you may need to give some attention to what you need to do when *you* run meetings.

You will be doing better if…

- You can recognise why some meetings you have attended did not achieve the desired results.

- You realise that your attitude towards a meeting can contribute to its success.

- You appreciate that meetings need to be managed properly.

- You know that if people are not comfortable, they will find it difficult to concentrate.

- You understand that people need to know what will be discussed at the meeting.

- You are clear about the objectives of any meeting that you run.

- You are certain that any meeting you initiate is really needed.

2 Meet with momentum

Meetings have a momentum of their own and will vary in pace, rhythm and mood. But because they bring people together as a group, they also exert another influence – one which imposes a more or less predictable pattern of behaviour on the participants.

Group processes

Before people attending the meeting can achieve anything of value, they need to learn to work together effectively. This process takes the form of four separate stages:

1 Forming: the settling-in stage

In this opening period, people need to get their bearings and also try to get the measure of each other in a polite way (since they have not yet found a reason to be rude to each other). They seek to know one another's attitudes and backgrounds and want to establish the ground rules, to help them settle in to the situation.

2 Storming: the boxing and coxing stage

Once people are more comfortable, they will start to open up. They may indulge in minor verbal skirmishes which can lead to the meeting becoming disorganised and quite difficult to control. This is the phase where people challenge each other. They are testing out their initial impressions, re-assessing them if necessary. This is an essential part of the process, as it clears the air.

3 Norming: the working productively stage
As meetings progress, ideas are developed and compromises reached, which involve alliances being made and deals being struck in order to get things moving forward. A framework is clearly established which enables everyone present to know what is expected of them.

4 Performing: the results-producing stage
At this final stage, people produce consensus and obtain results because they want to bring the meeting to a conclusion. Effective performance will now usually take precedence over everything else and constructive results will be achieved.

Understand the sequence of events
It is only in the last two phases that meetings can really begin to produce efficient and effective results. Should any decisions be made in either of the first two phases, they may well be half-baked and lacking in precision.

Meetings may operate at half power because people fail to work through some of the issues in the earlier stages. For example, some people may be pulling in different directions because they have not yet learned to co-operate or to appreciate each other's contributions.

Others might be using the meeting to achieve their personal and unstated aims as they may have hidden agendas.

How long each phase lasts depends on the people present and how well they know each other. If you can understand this sequence of events, this makes it easier to manage the pace of the meeting and prevent things from getting stuck in the earlier phases.

Group dynamics

When decisions are made by a group of people, they are often substantially different from those they would have made if they had been on their own.

This is because a form of herd instinct can come into play which persuades people to go along with the prevailing pressures. It can affect both the debate before decisions are made and also the decisions themselves.

Group pressure in debate

In groups, many people fear making fools of themselves. They become self-conscious about what they think, and often begin to doubt their own judgement. This pressure can have various effects. For instance:

- People who express doubts or question the validity of majority views can be pressurised into accepting the group consensus.

- People who take a stand may feel they will lose face if they concede, no matter how much evidence there is that they are wrong.
- People who may not be able to express their views coherently may end up agreeing by default.
- People who have doubts or differ in their views may tend to keep silent to avoid being seen to deviate from the group norm.

An apparent absence of objections may create an illusion of unanimity, yet this may not in fact truly represent the views of everyone who participated.

Group pressure in decision making

In groups, people can take decisions which exaggerate the initial positions of individual members.

This is known as 'the risky shift' and means that individual views within the group may become more extreme or more cautious as the meeting goes on. More often than not, group pressure can cause a shift towards greater risk. The type of shift generally depends on the dominant individual attitudes – ones which tend to have been formed well before the meeting takes place.

Riskier decisions may also be taken because individuals attending the meeting tend to feel that they are released from personal accountability, since no one person can be held wholly responsible for what is decided.

If the person running the meeting declares at the outset *'We ought to do 'X''*, the chances are that this is what will be agreed. As the whole purpose of most meetings is to discuss and exchange ideas, the polarising of entrenched views is counter-productive and can lead the group into making riskier decisions than are warranted.

Thus, if groups are to prove less vulnerable to these pressures and if they are to perform productively, it is vital that the person running the meeting remains impartial, encourages everyone to contribute, discusses every proposition and avoids expressing personal preferences.

Group forces

To make a meeting really productive it is necessary to take account of what is going on below the surface.

When a group of people meet they need to learn how to work together and for this they need to go through a process of forming, storming, norming, and ultimately, performing, in order to become a coherent and productive group.

Group pressure is brought to bear on individual thinking and decision-making and this can alter the dynamics of the meeting and sometimes lead to more risky outcomes than expected. When you are called upon to run a meeting, being aware of how groups develop and function makes it considerably easier to understand the range of underlying forces which may be at play.

Questions to ask yourself

Think about what can happen at meetings and answer the following questions:

- Do I appreciate that groups who attend meetings go through a number of dynamic stages before becoming fully productive?

- Am I aware of the extent to which individuals' behaviour can be affected by being in a group?

- Do I recognise that people may not proffer their real views because they are worried about what others will think?

- Do I understand that people may not change their minds, even when they wish to do so, for fear of losing face?

- Do I realise that silence does not necessarily mean agreement?

- Am I aware that people in groups may tend to make far riskier decisions than if they are asked to decide on their own?

You will be doing better if…

- You appreciate that there are four distinct stages in how people develop into a cohesive group and that only the final one is likely to produce effective results.

- You understand that individual thinking and behaviour can be affected by the group.

- You know that individuals can be pressurised into accepting group consensus.

- You are aware that some people cling to their opinions because they do not want to be seen to change their minds.

- You understand that a lack of dissent does not necessarily mean that there is consent.

- You appreciate that people in groups tend to make riskier decisions than they would as individuals.

- You realise that an awareness of group dynamics is valuable when running meetings.

You will be doing better if...

- You know what you are good at and can identify what your business does well.

- You know what you do not do so well.

- You know the areas that need improving within the business.

- You have worked out where your opportunities lie.

- You can envisage some of the ominous things that might materialise and prevent you from achieving your goals.

- You have worked out a contingency plan which will meet the worst of your fears.

- You have a clear and accurate picture of your current situation.

3 Organise meetings

The amount of care you give to how you organise a meeting contributes greatly to its success. There are several key things that you need to determine.

- What type of meeting it is.
- What it is about.
- Who needs to be present.
- Where and when it is to be held.

By spending a little time organising the meeting, this will help you to run the proceedings smoothly.

Types of meeting
Meetings, like dinner parties, can be formal or informal. It is best to know which type you are organising if things are to run smoothly.

Formal meetings
A formal meeting may be determined by its legal status or because the format has been laid down by certain rules and regulations. It may also require a specific number of attendees for its decisions to be recognised as constitutional.

Whatever its purpose, the points of procedure, not necessarily in this order, involve:

- **Agenda** What is to be discussed.
- **Minutes** The written record of the event.
- **Reports and recommendations** Supporting information and advice to assist in making decisions.
- **Debate** The general discussion.
- **Motions** What action is proposed.
- **Amendments** What modifications need to be made to a proposal.
- **Elections and voting** The acceptance or rejection of the motions.
- **Any other business** The issues which did not appear on the agenda.

It will be necessary to acquaint yourself with the rules *(often referred to as standing orders)* which apply to a formal meeting or you will not be able to run it properly, and any decisions made may not be considered valid.

Informal meetings
Informal meetings are much less constrained, but this does not mean they should be less structured. As a minimum, there should be:

- **An agenda** A list of topics to be discussed.
- **Someone to lead the meeting** A person responsible for running the meeting, even when it is the sort where jackets are discarded and feet put on tables.

- **A written outcome** A record of what is decided and who will be doing what as a result.

Informal meetings may be more relaxed in the way they are run and how people behave, but there is still a need to ensure that the proceedings are well-organised and the decisions recorded so that they end up being productive and move things forward.

Topics to be discussed

Every meeting should have some form of agenda. You need to appreciate that this is not a perfunctory piece of paper traditionally handed round before meetings like a free leaflet in the high street. Your agenda is a working document which acts as a compass to keep everyone on a specific course.

The main purpose of any agenda is to make sure the key items are fully addressed and to prevent the least important item taking up the most time. The sequence of the ideal agenda would look something like this:

- Purpose, date, time and place of meeting.
- Names of people attending.
- Routine topics for discussion.
- More difficult or controversial items.
- Any other business.
- The date of the next meeting.

The agenda determines the shape of the meeting. Your agenda needs to be constructed in such a way that it starts with the more straightforward areas for discussion and leads to the more difficult and usually critical aspects during the central part of the meeting. If you start with the uncontentious issues, you enable people to become involved from the start. It also means that once people have said 'yes', they tend to be more inclined to say 'yes' later on.

A helpful agenda is one which lets people know why the items are on the list by indicating what needs to be decided. This is not to be confused with deciding the outcome beforehand.

Sending out the agenda, even in draft form, prior to the meeting will give everyone an opportunity to prepare, and even to suggest additional items for discussion. It also gives you a chance to ask those who are invited to indicate whether they intend to come themselves or send someone else on their behalf.

People at the meeting

When convening meetings a good maxim to remember is 'less is more'. Two or three people frequently produce better results than a gathering of ten or twelve.

The more people attending the meeting, the more control and management are required. Should larger numbers of people be necessary, it is worth considering whether they all need to be at the meeting for the entire time, or whether they could arrive, make their contribution and leave again.

Who should attend the meeting will be determined by their requirement to:

- Make decisions and implement what has been agreed.
- Gather relevant information during the course of the meeting.
- Provide specific information.
- Influence the process of the meeting by providing necessary expertise, or at least peace-keeping skills.

Meetings are only as good as the people who attend them. If the wrong people are present, or key people are absent, it is highly unlikely that effective decisions will be made.

Whether people attend themselves or send a properly delegated proxy, it is essential to check that everybody who comes to the meeting has a reason and a purpose for being there.

Venue of the meeting

If only two or three are meeting, the venue can be quite relaxed and informal; a hotel lobby, a cubby-hole, or even a golf course. But if more than three people have a meeting, it really requires proper facilities, such as adequate heat, light, air, coffee/tea/water, no distractions, and at least the same number of chairs as there are people.

The two most important things, and ones which are often forgotten, are that:

- Everyone needs to be able to see everyone else.
- The person running the meeting needs to be able to make eye contact with everybody present in the room.

Where people sit is also worth considering if you want to ensure that the meeting will be productive. There are some simple things you can pre-plan when organising the venue where you are to hold the meeting. You need to:

- **Arrange the furniture** Make sure that everyone has a comfortable seat and can see everything.
- **Lay out the papers** Ensure everyone has the right papers for the meeting in front of them.

If people are not comfortable and cannot see each other or any visual aids and charts, they are unlikely to remain interested or attentive and may tend to sit doodling or day-dreaming from start to finish.

If there are two people who are known to be argumentative individuals, or who are known to take issue with each other, it may be wise to ensure that they do not sit beside, or directly opposite, each other. If you can place a belligerent individual next to a non-combatant, you will find that he or she is likely to be far less influential than if you allow like minds to congregate at one end of the table.

To ensure that people sit where you want them to, you can prepare a seating plan and place name cards in advance. Ask people to write their name on both sides of the cards so that the names face both inwards and outwards. While those seated know who they are, the others may not, particularly the person running the meeting.

Timetable

It is a good idea when considering the agenda to divide the time allocated for the meeting between the items, and keep a running total as the meeting progresses, for example:

- Item 1 – 10 mins [starting at 10.00]
- Item 2 – 15 mins [starting at 10.10]
- Item 3 – 20 mins [starting at 10.25]

This can always be amended as you go, but it allows you to move things along, and gives you a better chance of winding up the proceedings on time.

By taking time to plan the time to allocate to various items, you get an idea of which ones are likely to take the longest. You can also get an idea of how long the meeting is likely to last.

Meet successfully

It is said that over 80% of a meeting's success is determined before it takes place.

A relevant agenda is an essential constituent of any meeting, since it ensures people know in advance what the meeting is about.

When you give thought to who should attend the meeting, this also contributes considerably to its success. With the right people there, it is easier to get things decided.

Meeting in comfortable conditions enables everybody to concentrate on the subject matter, and apportioning time to each topic means that a plan exists to provide a framework for results.

Questions to ask yourself

Think about organising a meeting and ask yourself the following questions:

- Am I aware that running formal meetings requires me to follow predetermined rules?

- Do I appreciate that informal meetings still require a degree of formality?

- Do I understand the need to have an agenda?

- Do I confirm that the purpose of each meeting is clearly stated?

- Do I make sure the right people are invited to the meeting, and that they know why and when their presence is required?

- Do I arrange for meetings to be held in reasonably comfortable surroundings?

- Do I make certain that the layout of the meeting is such that everybody present can see everyone else?

- Do I set time limits on items for discussion?

You will be doing better if…

- You know the rules which apply to any formal meeting that you organise.

- You appreciate that informal meetings also need to be organised with some formality.

- You make certain that the agenda of the meeting is sent out in advance.

- You make sure that the right people attend.

- You ensure that the people attending know who the others are, and that everyone can see each other.

- You set time limits to each agenda item.

4 Control meetings

When it falls on you to run a meeting, there are several basic procedures to follow that will ensure that you conduct it effectively.

By opening the meeting positively and emphasizing the time constraints, you help people to focus their attention on the purpose of the meeting.

By directing the discussion and handling any disorderly conduct, you keep the meeting moving forward. Then by crystallising agreement and summarising the action, you can conclude the proceedings successfully.

Open the meeting

Once people have assembled, there are some important initial disciplines to observe which help set the tone for the ensuing meeting to be productive.

A warm welcome

Meetings which are started with a warm welcome being given to everyone participating usually start off on a crisp and positive note. If there are strangers present, consider asking everyone to introduce themselves (briefly) in turn, stating their name and title, before you introduce the first agenda item. If someone is to arrive late, or has to leave early, now is the time to say so, as this will reduce the effects of later disturbance.

Accept the minutes

If the meeting has reconvened, or is a standing committee, it is normal to accept the minutes or record of decisions taken at the last meeting.

Only in the most formal meetings will it be necessary to read out the previous minutes. And even then, it is far easier to ask, *'Does anyone have a problem with page 1?'* (Pause.) *'Page 2?'* And so on.

Discourage people from nit-picking over incorrect spelling or grammar unless it concerns the actual sense of the record. When you open the meeting in a positive manner, you set a positive tone and start things moving in the right direction.

Keep to time

Time-keeping is a major factor in meetings. From the moment everyone sits down, you need to keep a strict eye on the time and prevent it from being wasted. Some tried and tested methods for this are to:

- **Start on time** Even if some people have not yet arrived, it is important to stick to your schedule as this ensures people know that you intend to stick to your timings.
- **Calculate the cost of the meeting** Inform people of the amount it is costing to meet, having previously estimated how much each person present is earning and calculated what this means in terms of time.

'It's costing us a total of £900 to meet for one hour. This means £15 a minute, so let's make the best possible use of our time.'

- **Place an alarm clock in full view** Tell people that the clock is set to go off ten minutes before the due end of the meeting, so that you have time to summarise.
- **Have short breaks** This allows people to refocus and/or let off steam, especially if the meeting is going to be a long one.
- **Finish on time** People's attention can wane dramatically once you go over the allocated time. If business is concluded on time or earlier than scheduled, you will find this is usually very much appreciated.

It is important that everyone is made aware of the urgency of the meeting, so that time will not be squandered, and everyone feels that the person running the meeting is in control of the schedule.

Focus attention

At the start, it is always prudent to remind people what the meeting is to be about. This way you get them to focus their attention on what is going to be discussed.

To get people to focus, you need to:

- **State the existing situation or problem clearly** *'The situation is that we are rather overcrowded in the office.'*

- **Remind people of the purpose of meeting** *'The purpose of this meeting is to find a way to re-organise the available space.'*
- **Introduce the specific topic or topics to be discussed** *'Item 1 on your agenda concerns the location of the manuals which we all need to access, and which are presently kept behind the photocopying machine.'*

This stops people's attention from wandering, and enables them to focus on the points where decisions are required.

Direct the discussion

Once the meeting is under way, your principal function, as the person running the meeting, is to direct the discussion purposefully and prevent it departing from its aim. You need to:

- **Stick to the agenda** Unless it has been agreed that the order can be changed, state clearly which item on the agenda is about to be discussed. *'The next item to cover is Item 4.'*
- **Guide the meeting back to its objectives** If the meeting goes off course, it is vital you bring it back to its aims and direct people's energies to the business in hand. *'Can we remind ourselves what we are here for?' 'I don't think we want to get drawn into that issue...'*

Directing the discussion also means getting the best from those present by making sure that everyone plays his or her part and takes a positive interest in the proceedings. You need to:

- **Notice signs of withdrawal** If you see someone is staring vacantly into space, or has not spoken for quite a while, asking for an opinion will force the person to join in. *'Jim, have you anything to add to that?'* or *'Jane, what do you think of that suggestion?'*
- **Use the expertise of the group** By making use of the expertise of the people present enables others to make informed decisions. *'Fred, you were in charge of a similar situation. What was your experience when...?'*
- **Offer suggestions** By proposing ideas which contain possible courses of action encourages people to think creatively and helps to keep up the pace. *'Would it be a good idea to...?' 'Shall we discuss the possibility of...?'*
- **Support views** By endorsing other people's views and ideas, and by stating that you think their contributions are constructive, the discussion will be more productive. *'That could work really well,'* or *'Peter's idea sounds most promising. What do others think?'*

Intelligent direction of the discussion enables everyone to have their say and therefore find it easier to be more committed to the outcome.

Handle disorderly conduct

Meetings do not always advance in an orderly manner. Occasionally the conduct of individuals can impede progress and acrimonious exchanges can lead to head-to-head clashes.

Handling such conduct is stressful, but the role of the chairperson demands that you take control, however much you may dislike giving orders.

To take appropriate corrective action, you need to:

- **State clearly that personal attacks are unacceptable** *'Personal comments have no place in this meeting. Can we get back to the point, which is...'*
- **Ask for constructive suggestions** This can help counteract disagreement. *'Ted, if you don't agree with Bob, what do you suggest might solve this problem?'*
- **Move things forward** This is useful should opinions become argumentative. *'I appreciate there are strong feelings about this, but we need to move on. Perhaps the issue might be resolved by calling for a show of hands?'*

Reminding people of the meeting's objectives or making an appropriate light-hearted comment can also lower the temperature should things become fraught, and bring the meeting back to an even keel. *'Obviously, this is a subject that's close to your heart. Let's just take a few minutes to recap.'*

Disorderly conduct is rare, but thinking about how to handle it makes it easier to do so should the need arise.

Cope with diversions

People in meetings cannot help creating diversions, happily straying off course or going round and round, often in ever-decreasing circles. While this is far less stressful to cope with than disorderly conduct, it can also be far more exasperating.

This is where tact and diplomacy are required to get the meeting back on track and keep it moving forward. To do so you have to recognise and then cope with favourite forms of diversionary tactics. They may:

- **State difficulties** Listing the snags is meat and drink to some: *'We can't do that because...' 'That was tried last time and it didn't work.'* Asking for pertinent reasons why things cannot be done forces people to state their grounds for dissent in detail.
- **Have bees in bonnets** Some people will use any ruse to bring up their own obsession. Letting them have their say once, and then reminding them that they have already had their say, should stop them repeating themselves.
- **Go off at a tangent** Diverting the discussion into areas which are totally irrelevant is something some people do without realising it: *'Has anybody seen Volume II of*

the Oxford English Dictionary?' when the meeting is about where the reference books are to be located. Pointing out that this is not part of the topic under discussion prevents people from getting sidetracked and brings the meeting back on course.

By not allowing people to divert or disrupt the meeting through using tactful and diplomatic guidance, you ensure that things will move forward positively.

Crystallise agreement

As the meeting progresses, you need to move things forward and crystallise the discussion so that the meeting can come to a consensus. This is a critical part of the meeting, because if you do not have agreement, little will be accomplished afterwards.

It is important to make sure that a conclusion is reached. To do this, you need to:

- **Review points of agreement and disagreement** Identify where people agree and highlight where they disagree. This pinpoints those things which still have to be agreed. Sum up the progress of the meeting as you see it. *'So we all agree about..., but we still have to resolve...'*
- **Ask questions to check your understanding** When you ask questions you not only ensure that you know exactly what's what but also you can clarify other

people's grasp of certain issues when they may not have been bold enough to ask. *'Do you mean that...?' 'Just let me check that I have understood...'*

- **State intermediate conclusions** Round up points as they are dealt with. This provides a résumé of the proceedings so far and makes people feel that, even before the end of the meeting, it is producing results. *'Let's just run through what we've agreed. For Item 2, everyone considers that the best course to take will be...'*

- **Make sure that there is general acceptance** Monitor that there is agreement so that you can forge ahead to the next point. *'Can I just check that we're all happy with this decision?' 'Has anyone anything further to add on this item before we move on?' 'Is everyone agreed?'*

This allows you to keep track of how people are thinking and act as a referee if required. It also enables decisions to accrue, so that it is easier to reach a final result.

As things are agreed, it is prudent to record them at the time. This prevents you having to go over various points at a later stage and possibly finding that someone has had a change of heart, or was never in favour of a particular decision in the first place.

By making sure that people fully concur with what has been agreed at the time it was agreed prevents the issue from being resurrected and possibly disrupting another part of this meeting – or perhaps even the next one.

Recap for action

At the end of the meeting, it is essential to ensure that everyone is committed to the decisions taken.

If meaningful and productive action is to follow, there must be an overall and final reminder of what has been agreed during the course of the meeting. You need to:

- **Summarise conclusions clearly** This leaves people in no doubt about what has been decided. They cannot later claim they were unaware of what was agreed. *'I am now going to summarise this meeting. We met to discuss the problem of space in the office. What has been decided is as follows. Firstly, we decided... Finally, we decided that the best place for the reference books would be the reception area.'*
- **Agree on tasks and time limits** This leaves no doubt as to who will do what and by what date. *'It was agreed that Jim will organise ... by the 30th May and liaise with Jill, who is going to...'*

The summary is crucial. If the action that has been agreed is not clearly stated, very little will happen and all the time and effort can easily be wasted.

A properly run meeting is one where people feel things have been decided. They know what they have do and feel more confident that something will definitely happen as a result of the meeting.

Keep control

Whatever form meetings take and whatever their purpose, it is up to the person running them to be clear about what needs to be achieved and to keep that aim in view at all times.

The role is not unlike that of a sheep dog, having to herd its flock into a pen. The sheep may try to stray, but constant checking and chivvying keeps them moving in the right direction.

It is vital to sum up the main conclusions of the meeting, so that action can result.

Questions to ask yourself

Think about how you run meetings and answer the following questions:

- Do I open the meeting in a positive way?

- Do I make sure that meetings always start on time?

- Do I remind people what the meeting is about?

- Do I stick to the agenda and guide people back to it when things stray off course?

- Do I keep order gently but firmly?

- Do I enable everyone to have their say?

- Do I make sure that everyone agrees with what has been agreed at the time it is agreed?

- Do I summarise the conclusions and make sure everyone knows who is doing what?

You will be doing better if...

- You appreciate that meetings need direction if they are to produce results.

- You start your meetings on time, even if somebody has not yet turned up.

- You work through the agenda systematically and cover all items.

- You let everyone have their say, within limits.

- You stop argument from escalating.

- You bring the discussion back on track.

- You make sure that everyone is in agreement with the decisions made at the time they are made.

- You summarise the outcomes and indicate who is responsible for further action and by what time.

- You focus on ensuring that the meeting produces results.

5 Document the meeting

A meeting needs to be accurately documented so that you know precisely what was agreed and specifically who is committed to doing what.

If you are wise, you should also try to gauge opinion about how the meeting went, so you can improve the way you run the next one or make sure that you repeat your competent performance from this one.

Record the meeting

It is neither practical nor desirable for the person running the meeting to record the proceedings as well. In certain instances, it may require a professional secretary or rapporteur to take the minutes.

Concentrating on controlling the discussion is a full-time job, so it is best if someone else is assigned to record the meeting's progress and its outcome. When choosing someone to do this, you need to bear in mind what is expected from the role.

During the meeting

During the meeting, it is important to make sure that there is someone who is appointed to:

● **Note the key points** Match these against each agenda item, as to what was agreed and who will do it.

- **Advise on procedure** *(especially for formal meetings)* Know the conventions you need to follow.
- **Have previous meeting records to hand** Along with spare agendas, these can be handed out to those who turn up without them.
- **Keep an eye on the time allocated for each item** It helps if a subtle method of communicating time constraints can be agreed before the meeting begins.

There is seldom a requirement for a verbatim record so, when making notes, the trick is to reach a balance between recording everything that is said and jotting down the odd note.

This means ensuring that the person recording the meeting knows that the task is to listen carefully to what is said, and to note only the basic details and key phrases together with the initials of the speaker in order to attribute the right things to the right people.

After the meeting

Once the meeting is concluded, the notes taken need to be turned into a formal written record of the proceedings. It is wise to see that this done as soon as possible after the meeting while events are still fresh in the mind. (Making it up later is not an option.)

The record (or minutes) should contain the following essential information:

- A heading indicating what the meeting was about and the date and time it was held.
- A list of the people present.
- Apologies from those who did not attend.
- A précis of what was decided about each agenda item, and who made what significant contribution.
- A summary against each item of who will do what.

Writing the record requires the proceedings of the meeting to be presented briefly in an objective and business-like style. You need to:

- **Use reported speech** Write in the past tense, *'Jim Smith pointed out that...' 'Jane Brown said this was not a problem because...' 'It was decided to...'*
- **Describe the proceedings factually** Do not give personal opinions about what happened.
- **Indicate any action to be taken** Use bold type or have a separate column where appropriate action is listed beside the initials or job titles.

Before the minutes are finally issued, you need to check that the account is authentic. It makes a nonsense of the whole event if inaccurate reporting leads to subsequent misunderstandings.

It helps to keep in mind that the record is not an end in itself; it acts as a spur to action. Whatever form it takes, the sole purpose of the record is to ensure that people have no excuse not to know what went on or what they have agreed to do.

Evaluate the Meeting

It is rare for meetings to be evaluated. Most people who run meetings are only too grateful that it is all over and that they got through it unscathed. But the skills involved in chairing a meeting are best developed through actually running them.

The best way to do better at meetings is to get feedback from the people there on how they thought the meeting went. If you are running meetings regularly, it is helpful to find out how you are doing by asking whether others think that you are achieving results.

And a simple way of doing this is to request those attending to fill in a short, pre-prepared form before they leave, one that only takes a minute or so to complete. Ask them to complete this before they leave the meeting.

The sort of things that you might ask are:

- Was this meeting of use to you?   Yes/No
- Did you manage to say all you needed to?   Yes/No
- Were you satisfied how the meeting was run?   Yes/No
- Do you know what you are going to do
  as a result of this meeting?   Yes/No
- Do you have any other comments?   Yes/No

Getting answers to these questions, even if no-one has the time to write anything under 'any other comments', enables you to evaluate how well they think you have run the meeting and, if necessary, what to do better next time.

Have evidence

Recording the proceedings is a key activity. Without written evidence it can only be recalled by hearsay and memory, neither of which is reliable.

The record needs to be succinct and should be written sooner rather than later. It should be viewed as a prompt to all those attending to act on the decisions made. Therefore the clearer the record, the more likely others are to take note of what they are supposed to be doing, and the more likely it is that the meetings you run will result in action.

Questions to ask yourself

Think about how you go about organising the recording of the meeting and answer the following questions:

- Do I work productively with the person recording the meeting?

- Are all the key points of discussion noted and attributed?

- Are the major decisions recorded?

- Is the record written up as soon after the meeting as possible?

- Do I make sure only facts were reported, and not personal opinions?

- Do I check the final version of the minutes before they are issued?

- Do I think the record is an accurate account of what happened at the meeting?

You will be doing better if…

- You are fully supported by the person recording the meeting.

- You find that the minutes give a succinct and objective account of the meeting.

- You find that the key decisions taken at the meeting have been accurately recorded.

- You are satisfied that the action to be taken by everyone attending the meeting has been clearly identified.

- You check the accuracy of the record while events are fresh in your mind.

- You believe that the record accurately reflects the proceedings.

6 Your attitude to meetings

For meetings to be productive, not only do you have to be skilled at running them, you also require to adopt a positive attitude. By playing your part, taking charge, meeting expectations and doing what is assigned to you, you ensure that you get the best out of meetings and this behaviour reinforces your positive attitude.

Take charge

You have it in your power to make a meeting effective, but to do this, you need to be prepared to take charge. If you do not, you should not expect much to come of the meeting. To take charge means you need to:

- **Assume authority** Remind yourself that your role gives you the authority to control the meeting.
- **Take charge** Give yourself permission to take charge of the proceedings, even if it seems a bit like laying down the law.
- **Enjoy it** Convince yourself that you can do it and that you are going to enjoy it.

People attending the meeting look to you for a lead and expect you to take charge of the proceedings. Since they cannot do so themselves, you will be jeopardising the meeting if you do not.

Expect the best

If you have high expectations of the meeting, it is very likely to achieve a high level of results.

You need to translate your expectations into practical terms by adopting a positive attitude. There are several beliefs that you need to hold to make this happen. These include believing that:

- **The meeting is important** Because if you do not think this, then perhaps you should not be running it.
- **The people attending it are necessary** Because if you do not believe that everyone present needs to be there, you may find it difficult to give credence to their ideas and suggestions.
- **The time will be well spent** Because if you do not think you are spending your time profitably, you will communicate this very clearly by your behaviour.
- **Good will come of it** Because if you do not anticipate achieving good results from the meeting, you will have programmed yourself to accept that nothing will come of it, and the odds are that nothing will.

The attitude you bring with you on arrival at a meeting establishes the tone at the outset. If you instantly unload your pressure on others, *'It couldn't be a worse time for this meeting,'* this will not only depress everyone within earshot, but unleash other expressions of despondency.

But if you look optimistic and make a few good-humoured and interested comments as people are settling down, the meeting will have a better chance of starting, and thus continuing, in a positive spirit.

Take action

It is the sum total of the collective effort that determines the success of the meeting. If you do not carry out the tasks assigned to you, and others opt out as well, very little will be achieved.

To make sure something happens after the meeting, you need to:

- **Read the minutes** This verifies what you are required to do and to note what others will be doing.
- **Work out how to get things done** Consult and work with the agreed timescale, and delegate what you can to others who are capable of doing this.
- **Take action** It is up to you to some something, rather than hope that you will be released from your responsibilities.

Putting things in hand while the impetus of the meeting is still with you almost guarantees that you will get them done. It also prevents you from being tempted to sidle out of your obligations. If you do your bit and others do so too, then the meeting will have been an unqualified success.

Be productive

The attitude you take to the meetings you run will do a lot to determine whether they will be productive or not.

There is little point running a meeting if you do not intend it to achieve anything. This is just a waste of everyone's time and energy. The more you expect meetings to achieve, the more productive you will find them and the more you will be rewarded.

If you are seen to be totally focused on getting results, others will take their cue from you and, if everyone gives the meeting their full attention, a successful outcome is more or less guaranteed. At the very least, you should never hear others complain about any meeting you have run being a waste of time.

Questions to ask yourself

Think about your attitude to any meeting you run and
answer the following questions:

- Do I expect the meeting to achieve results?

- Do I communicate my positive attitude to others?

- Do I believe the meeting is worthwhile?

- Do I have confidence in my ability to run a meeting
  efficiently?

- Do I take charge of the meeting?

- Do I take charge of the proceedings when this is called
  for?

- Do I do what I am supposed to do after the meeting?

You will be doing better if...

- You have high expectations of the meeting.

- You communicate your positive attitude to others.

- You consider every meeting you run to be important and worth your time.

- You believe in your ability to make the meeting effective.

- You take charge of the meeting from the outset.

- You exert your authority.

- You anticipate good results.

- You read and act upon the minutes immediately after the meeting.

Check your progress

If you are finding that meetings are proving to be less productive than you think they should be, consider whether this could possibly be because you may have failed to take account of one or more of the following aspects:

Understand the dynamics of meetings

If you find it difficult to understand why people behave as they do when you are running meetings, perhaps you have not fully appreciated that there are predictable phases that groups need to experience in order to become productive. Maybe you did not give proper consideration to the pressure placed on individuals by group influences, which can make them behave very differently from the way they would if they were deciding on their own.

Organise the meeting

If the meeting does not begin on time, if the items for discussion are carried out in no particular order, if no-one is designated to run or record the proceedings, and if the coffee never arrives, it is clearly a lack of organisation that is causing the problem. Without an agenda sent out in good time, people cannot come fully prepared. Without proper preparation beforehand, you cannot expect the meeting to produce results.

Control the meeting

If meetings seem to overrun their allotted time, discussion is unresolved before the next item is reached, nobody is clear about how a decision was arrived at or what bearing it has on their actions, then you may not have taken charge of the meeting. Maybe you are not keeping control of the conversation and have allowed it to stray too far from its aims. Possibly you are not making sure that points are clarified and agreed as you go along. Or it could be that you are not leaving yourself enough time to summarise who should do what at the end.

Document the meeting

If the record of the meeting is not all it should be, possibly you did not explain what you required of the minutes, so there is too much padding, or perhaps the presentation is poor. Or maybe it does not contain all the salient facts, or these are inaccurate because the record was compiled too long after the event.

Your attitude to meetings

If you regard running a meeting as a chore and do not expect it to achieve a great deal, you can hardly be surprised if it does not. You need to be convinced that, as the person who is running the meeting, it is your positive attitude that makes the difference between failure and success.

Reap the benefits

Meetings are an integral part of managing anything. It is important to bear in mind that to have results, they need to be well run. And to run them well, you need to know what needs to be done and have confidence in doing it.

The benefits of running good meetings are that:

- People are better informed.
- People have a forum to express their views.
- People can explore and assess ideas.
- Agreement is reached.
- Decisions are made, even if they are decisions to take no decision.
- People are more likely to accept the decisions because they have been part of the decision-making process.
- Action is taken.
- Things get done.

Getting people involved in what is happening is a good way to gain their commitment to taking action. By running your meetings effectively, you will prompt this to happen.

Glossary

Here are some definitions in relation to how you can run effective meetings.

Agenda
> *A list of items to be discussed or business to be transacted, preferably in the best possible order to achieve the objectives.*

Chairperson/man/woman, or just **Chair**
> *The person running the meeting; vital, with or without the title.*

Control
> *Regulate the tempo and temperature of the meeting in order to produce results.*

Disruption
> *Anything that interrupts the rhythm of the meeting from phone bleeps to a full-scale row.*

Diversion
> *Anything that people would rather talk about than the main issue, and which has to be curbed at all costs.*

Group
> *A number of people considered as a collective unit; rather more than the sum total of individuals in it.*

Item
> *Subject for discussion or consideration. Try not to have too many.*

Meeting

A means to an end. Not to be forgotten.

Minutes

Official record of the proceedings.

Motion

A formal proposal, without the ring or the roses.

Preparation

A state of readiness. Make sure you have done your homework before attending.

Points of procedure

The rules and regulations of formal meetings (a.k.a. standing orders).

Purpose

The whole reason for the meeting. It's important to remember why you are attending any meeting.

Quorum

The minimum number of members required at the meeting in order to transact business.

Result

The outcome, which, if not constructive, merely consists of fixing another meeting.

Secretary/Rapporteur

A designated professional recorder of the minutes who should need no telling how to take them.

Summary

Brief synopsis of the main points to remind people what they decided.

Further reading

Run meetings provides you with an overview of the basic skills you need to develop to help you run productive and useful meetings.

Below are some other resources which you might find useful when seeking to develop and enhance your skills when running meetings further.

Alan Barker (2011)
How to Manage Meetings (Creating Success), 2nd Edition, London: Kogan Page.

Harvard Business School Press (2006)
Running Meetings: Expert Solutions to Everyday Challenges, Boston Massachusetts: Harvard Business School Publishing.

Duncan Peberdy (2009)
Brilliant Meetings What to Know, Say and Do to Have Fewer, Better Meetings, Harlow: Pearson Business.

About the author

Kate Keenan, CPsychol, AFBPsS, BA, BSc, MSc, MPhil, has over 20 years experience as a chartered psychologist and is expert in the areas of occupational and organisational psychology. Kate specialises in promoting psychological wellbeing in the workplace. She has worked extensively with corporate and independent businesses, devising strategic management programmes that enable them to identify and resolve managerial issues – from personnel selection and individual assessment to team building and attitude surveys.

She also works as a mentor and coach, offering a series of practical and transformative evidence-based strategies designed to help people make the most of their opportunities, both business and personal. In particular, she helps entrepreneurs and business owners maximise their prime asset – themselves.

Kate has a post-graduate qualification in Mental Health Studies from Kings College, London and currently lives in Bath.

In terms of being able to **run meetings**, she says:

'I quite enjoy attending meetings, but confess to a degree of trepidation about running them myself. However, by remembering to focus on the pertinent issues, meetings seem to have a better than average rate of covering all the ground and finishing on time with fully determined follow-up actions.'

Pocket Manager Books

'Especially for people who neither have the time nor the inclination for ploughing through the normal tomes...'

The Daily Telegraph

Personal development
- Assert yourself [65]
- Handle stress
- Make time
- Manage yourself

Essential business skills
- Manage
- Plan
- Recruit
- Run meetings
- Solve problems

Productive relationships
- Communicate
- Delegate
- Motivate
- Negotiate
- Understand people

More information about these books available at...
www.kate-keenan.com

Proof

Made in the USA
Charleston, SC
25 March 2015